Poems from the Mind Of a Madman

Poems from the Mind Of a Madman

Passionate Works of Poetry For Modern Times

Don J. Metivier

AuthorHouse™
1663 Liberty Drive
Bloomington, IN 47403
www.authorhouse.com
Phone: 1-800-839-8640

First published by AuthorHouse 03/26/2015

ISBN: 978-1-4634-1381-1 (sc)
ISBN: 978-1-4634-1379-8 (hc)
ISBN: 978-1-4634-1377-4 (e)

Library of Congress Control Number: 2011908854

Print information available on the last page.

This book is printed on acid-free paper.

CONTENTS

Political War

Political, Government, War
Bleeding soldiers at the core
No talks in Afghanistan
First Iraq, next Korea, and then Iran

We lay our waste where we can
As part of our democratic plan
Fed rotted remnants of what we see
Misinformed, misled by our own country

When I was in service I came to believe
We've the mightiest country with tricks up its sleeves
They promise citizens, soon the wars will end
Unseen, more soldiers they continue to send

Expendable pawns in their game of chess
Made to feel irreplaceable with a little tenderness
Threatened to follow the general order
Like lambs to the slaughter, we cross another border

Good men and women who want to do right
Willing to die in some nameless fight
As long as the power reaches it's goal
The lives of our troops will take its toll

The dead are heroes the living unknown
Thousands of lives made of flesh and bone
To God, to unit, to family, to some Semper Fi
To my country . . . tell us the truth before they die

All Seasons Fall

October's crescent moon, with its dim autumn glow
From here, far below, she shines with an ochre hue
As evenings cool down to new temperatures low
The early fog rises across valleys topped with morning dew
As I look out in reflection at the haze, I think "what a view!"

Crops all set to harvest, like sweet corn by the row
Ah, New England ripe-red apples with a flavor so right
All around colors abound, crimson maples and birch yellow
Burnt cedar-wood aroma smoke fills the night, such delight
Warming my senses in the clear, crisp star-filled night

Homes welcome others with their jack-o-lantern décor
Winds brush the grass tops as the fields turn to gold
Hay bales piled in barns, sheltered from rains sure to follow
Children in bed, telling stories like *The Legend of Sleepy Hollow.*
Such tales won't hold the same thrill tomorrow, I say with sorrow . . .

Filled with masquerades, scarecrows, candy and Indian corn
Another fall season highlights with All Hallows Eve
Villages take folly in all manners of superstitions born
As we take time to remember, let go in hopes of our souls reprieve
On this note, I for one must assuredly conceive, I believe

Tall-ships seek harbor, as the wind witch starts to blow
Graveyards turn ghostly as moonlit stone shadows lie still
However, soon Octobers fall maiden will be covered in a blanket of snow
Turned winters leafless tree sentinel, sitting alone on a distant hill
Though all seasons must surely fall, I wish time would stand still

Civility

Snare drum rolls
Patriot with a fife
The death tolls
Waste of life

Dressed in blue
Adorned in grey
Nothing to say to you
Nothing left to say

Blood red fields
Walls of stone
No wound heals
When you're dying alone

I "Grant" you peace
I surrender you "Lee"
Let this battle cease
Ending slavery

For whom will you kill?
Who shall you take away?
You can't talk without will
Cast out pride and pray

A Simple Touch

Feeling a leaf fall
Gently against your face
Touching your soul
You've been touched by grace

A sign from heaven
Sent your way
Wakes the senses
What a beautiful day!

Led to higher ground
Sheltered in the stone
Gentle wind blows around
Silence, you're alone

Ah, choose the path
To whom you are
You're a star in knowing
There's billions glowing

A chance to choose one
Places your mind at ease
Your light touching everyone
Like leaves, falling from trees

The Flower That Could Be

Poor petal flower that could not grow
Denied of the water that gives you life
Hidden from the sunlight that lights your way
Keeping true, holding your blossom for another day

Poor petal flower that would not grow
Kept from the rich soil that feeds you
Eaten by insects that feed on your whole
Staying true you're beautiful colors yet to unfold

Poor petal flower that wishes to grow
Unnourished center and empty inside
Roots that have seeded but not taken hold
Being true, to find the way out of the dark and cold

I am that flower . . .

If But For A Telepathic Moment

You move closer, she moves farther away
Smiling eyes speak, like they've something to say
Not a word spoken, only thoughts cross the space
Exchanged casual glances, your heart starts to race

Seconds pass by, then she turns away
Your mind starts to speak, you wish her to stay
Your lips starts to move, but nothing comes out
Then, as though she heard you, she turns about

Chocolate Lover

I love to eat wonderful chocolate
I always carry it in my pocket
My favorite passion to be sure
There's not an illness it won't cure

When I'm down and out I eat it
It makes me feel better again, complete
I think it's even better than sex
It's surely my strongest complex

All brown, white and sugary sweet
Silky smooth, oh my, what a treat!
My personal best is darkest and pure
But, white and milky have their allure

Oh chocolate, grown in many places
Bitter beans put smiles on people's faces
With pods of green and brown
It's the best thing going around

Don't forego cocoa served hot or cold
Brewed just right, flavorful and bold
A drink coffee lovers might never know
Oh chocolate, luscious chocolate, I love you so.
Call me your chocolate lover!

In Interest

I surround myself with strange, esoteric things
Things I believe in, like old secrets hiding in the wings
Fairies, floating and dancing around
Cryptids, Djinn and lights moving with no sound
Magic forgotten and passed down lore
Numerology, calming scent and some magic door
Other dimensions we don't see, the number three
Serendipity, instinct and eventuality
Mind-reading, time travel and karma
Singing bowls, quartz energy and the Dali Lama
Crop circles, energy lines and UFO's
Spirits and levitation, no one really knows
Angels versus demons, evil versus good
Ancient chambers, mysterious monks with hood
Jersey Devil, Loch Ness Monster and Lake Champlain
The Ark of Covenant and bloody rain
The power of sound, the Holy Grail
The Shroud of Turin's blood from the nails
Alchemy, sacrifice, potions and spells
Heaven, near death, purgatory and different hells
Noah's Ark lying on Mount Ararat
The Templar's Treasure, the vampire bat
Undecipherable tablets and crystal skulls
Blackbeard's booty and exploding seagulls
Laying on of hands and healing stones
Curses, Ouija boards and throwing bones
Meditation, visualization and musical brain power
Halloween, scarecrows and the witching hour
Creepy crawlies, scary clowns, The Siren sings
Graveyard anomalies and gargoyles with wings
With all of these wonders to keep me intrigued
It's no wonder my mind is always fatigued

Alien Denial

Pulsating light
Withering green
Things in the night
Very often seen

Silent reflection
Glimmering black
No protection
Knowledge we lack

Under a mirror
Who's seeing who?
Nothing could be clearer
Than events true

Brilliant white flash
Lost and standing
Covered in ash
Signs of a landing

No one seems to believe
When it is spoken
A mind won't conceive
History, left broken

So long we don't see
Nothing to fear
Eyes of alien company
We all know are here

The Curious House

There on the path, an old wooden fence
When initially seen, stands as though in defense
Observed, it's just a broken picket wall
Leaning, showing signs of its soon demise and fall
Quite quaint I'd say and inviting in some way
As though a passer-by, as I would be welcomed to stay
Uneven crooked flagstones lead to a door
Of a bungalow with a heart at its core
Old paint that is chipping, a bluish hue
Wounded by time, a missing slat or two
A white columned porch invites one to sit
Weather-worn gray floor boards provide it
Upon one's passing in view, a curtained window
Sits directly above an open cellar hole, below
The curtained window shows someone lives here
Though upon inspection, it's a mystery with such disrepair
The roof is disheveled, the chimney missing bricks
The yard un-kept with overgrown hemlocks and its sticks
With no driveway possible or place for a car
I'd imagine the only way to town was a bicycle by far
On the opposite side of the frontal path are tall old trees
Each reaching dead branches towards the houses eaves
The effect is such as to create a secret hollow
The cause of interest would make anyone follow
Time to walk in the hollow, as a passer on his way
For to stay too long and delay my memories, I'd overcome my stay
I write this now, because I remember the day
When I fell upon this curious little house, while on my way

Isolation

Sometimes you think it's over
That's when it starts all over again
Sometimes you wonder where you are
You wonder if you'll reach an end

Sometimes you're not sure of tomorrow
At times, you're not sure of today
You hang on but fill up with sorrow
You wonder, you seek, you pray

So many serious issues to deal with
Too many problems you have to resolve
You seek answers in your tool kit
For a god, or a friends to involve

But, you want to be alone
As your pride starts to spill
You don't answer the phone
But you think, soon you will

Sometimes you think it's over
Then, life starts all over again
There's no need to wonder who you are
You're a person and you just need a friend

My Beautiful Flower . . . Holly Anne

My colorful flower of love . . .
You blossom towards the sky above
How you spread a colorful rainbow
Shining bright, your softly lit petals glow

What a wonderful, beautiful gift you bestow
On all those that take part as you grow
Sturdy leaves, calming shades of forest green
Emerging, emitting a soft, supple waxy sheen

Strongly, stem-rooted to the ground
On a plush green carpeted mound, you resound
You're visited by bees and butterflies
That spread your goodness via the skies

You're sunlit center of fruitful seeds
Take hold and sprout about life's weeds
O dormant beauty in the quiet night
Unfolding magic in the morning light
. . . Such a magnificent sight, truly love's delight.

The Bike Game

Young boys playing games
Games they created by names
Just two blocks from home
Invincible and left on their own

They'd take turns as to who's the one
That's part of the fun
So the others run and hide
The one on a bicycle starts to ride

Seeking out his concealed friends
Once all were found, they'd start again
They all know the hour is getting late
But, as a group ruling, they decide to wait

Maybe time for one more game to play
After all, they'd waited for this all day
But, time doesn't wait that way
Darkening out, as the sun fades away

Then comes a heartbreaking shout
One by one, their names are called out
Still, they make time to laugh and say goodbye
Each carried home by their parent's cry

Today, these young warriors have all grown
Alliance dismantled, each gone on their own
Though, each member has gone their way
Something remains in each, a yesterday

The happiness in this old man's story
Is in knowing these boys can relive their glory
As each ages and lives their lives beyond
What made them strong forever will carry on

Finding Home

As the season turns to snow
She'll board a plane in Chicago
Heading West to where the sun sets low
She will bask in its warm afterglow
Yeah, bask in its warm afterglow

She will leave the cold for the warm
Feel the calm, not the winter's storm
Avoid the chill she's felt for so long
At last, she believes her problems gone
Yeah, at last her problems are gone

Young lady, building her cozy nest
Trying to live with a sunny zest
Try hard as she might, her very best
Still, she lives in a state of unrest
Yeah, still lives in a state of unrest

As time falls back to longer days
Memories reflect in the sunny haze
Haunting of a cold and windy place
She'd left in our good God's grace
Yeah, left in our good God's grace

Warm to the bone, now growing old
The end of her life starts to unfold
Soon, her life will be a story told
She tried to leave the northern cold
Yeah, tried to leave the northern cold

Inside her a feeling starts to grow
There's a place called home, she'll go
So, as the golden rays slowly set below
She boards a plane back to Chicago
Yeah, boards a plane back to Chicago

It's here, she'll settle down at last
As her last winter comes to pass
Sun shines on the snow in contrast
She now lies warm, under the snow-covered grass
Yeah, warm under the cold covered grass

Providence, Rhode Island

Towering buildings
Fountain in the middle
Many things
Of which I know so little

Gilded domes
Where pigeons roam
Central, reaching trees
With wilted leaves

A busy place
Cars, speeding by
People walk, rushing
In this crowed space

River fire runs right through
Something to see if I were you
Where two elements diverge
Opposing, yet converge. True!

Bridges and crossways and lines
Sculpture, art and displays
A famous school of design
One big diverse cultural mind

I look and then I see
Oh, a sight that pleases me
Couples engaging in love
A young couple, seemingly

It's providence we all seek
Here, Providence is found
Our city we shall keep
To be safe and sound

Waiting Room

Long lines and rails
Hurry to no avail
Waiting room with a TV
Places so all can see
If you look you'll find
This limbo is a design
A timeless space
Where you sit or pace
Where children drive you mad
Make you agitated, a tad
With chairs constructed in such a way
Uncomfortably built so you don't stay
But, stay you must until your name is called
Till you hear your name echo in the hall
Paneling, desks with busy hosts
People walk by you like ghosts
Each waits and wears their own face
All just casual glances in this space
Now and then someone will talk
A viewpoint, complaint or just a balk
Sometimes someone gets up and leaves
Usually disgruntled, yes one can see
With only so much time and something to do
This uncomfortable place gets to you

Felled Tree

Fallen tree
Fallen tree
What was it
That felled thee

Still stately
That, I see
Still rooted
Partially

While weak muscle
Leaves still rustle
Creatures still roam
A changed home

Arms still reach
Branches still breach
A forest of green
What a sight to be seen!

I'm blessed I see
To have found this tree
For as it's life fades away
I see myself in a new way

If Only I Could Live in a Dream

I'm fed up today
I suffice to say
At everyone, everything, in everyway
Nothing's going to make it o.k.
God knows, I'm not going to pray
He knows I'd be lying anyway

My thoughts would make a shrink think
There's something in my cellar making a stink
Some buried bones, from long ago
Buried deep in the ground, so no one would know
Not a time for the weary to venture below
You may find what you seek, then "oh no!"

Last night, I had some crazy dreams
I had the best of times it seems
Sex like I've never had and laser beams
Pleasure like eating fine chocolates and creams
Then, I woke up to the sound of worker's machines

No wonder I'm fed up today
I suffer to say.

Mother (For Doris)

A mother is there when you don't expect her there
She appears in the night to calm your fear
A word from her is all it takes
"Stay awake little child, I'll calm the shakes"
Sickness, worry, casualty and pain
Shelters you from sunlight an covers you in rain
A smile can turn a cloudy day
A mother is there when it needs to go away
Mother doesn't expect from you
But, she does ask you to be true
A mother is your whole world always
If there is no more time, she stays
Mother cooks great cakes and pies
There's nothing mother can't if she tries
She says, it's going to be alright
A calming thought when your mind is in a fight
Guiding you through school, hugging you good
Even a failed test or task she would
When is seems all is just out of reach
She divides herself, same to each
We love our mother because of our connection
It times of difficulty, or happiness she is in the reflection
She grows old and you want her to be there
How can you return the lifetime of care?
She doesn't expect you to and is sincere
The things you did, if only you could repair
Mother knows that things happen for a reason
That life is full of fulfillment each season
When the time comes and mother must go
She has given you love and all you'll ever know
Mother is loved, living in our hearts place
Mother is gone and you hold onto her grace
She has made you a special part of the human race

A Sparkle of Time

Rational thinking or creative reasoning
Inbred genetics or years of seasoning
A moment can happen so undersigned
Mindful eyes that look can see a thing

Like today, just some snow falling gently
Brushing, tickling, touching my head
As the wind began pushing me away
I turned towards it instead

A preponderance of emotions
Suddenly enveloped me
I stood alone with my trusty dog
By my side, faithfully

He may not have been as discerning
To this singular moment at hand
Or, perhaps his heart was aquiver as mine
Overwhelmed as we took our stand

We stood at a tree line of pines
Not a soul to be seen all around
The quiet of winter was giving a sign
Powdery flakes of wonder, traveling to the ground

Simple yes, but enough to send a shiver down my spine
The engraved snapshot in the mind
In the millions of snowflakes, we were there
The reality of sharing a sparkle of time

Music

New music starts to ring
In my ears it sings
Alive with notes of harmony
Designed with beats of simplicity

A little laughter makes me smile
The music makes it all worthwhile
Volume keeps just the right tone
I attach to each ear a headphone

The music and I are now one
The melding of rhythms has begun
It's personalized, simple and true
You store in your emotional queue

A beautiful place, where there's no pain
Pleasure senses open in the brain
Places and memories to visit again
Music brings calm and peace like a friend

Maybe, if the world listened to music more
We'd see there's nothing worth fighting for
Music is something we all can share
I'd give all my music to those who would hear

Let the winds of angels wings
Carry the joy that all music brings
To the poor, the suffering, the lost
God knows we need healing right now
. . . At all costs!

Colors I Don't See

Beyond a horizon of blue and green, hides a world unseen
A dimensional world beyond what's visible, colors my eyes don't see
Ah, but what a blessed man I am, surrounded by colors around me
Oh, I'd like to see the other invisible colors, that I am sure glow
Like brilliant stars in the distant sky, but why should I?
In the world I can see, I'm engulfed in a magical rainbow
This is the world I'm meant to know, otherwise the other would show
So, I'll admire all objects around me and take comfort in their shine
I'll live in the light of the present, enjoying this life that's mine
Thus, let the unseen live in spirit, still I know it's all around me
As real as my reality before me, beyond the blue sky and green tree

Observation

An observation is clear
A change can suddenly appear
For me, I noticed a change in the bees
They've become more aggressive recently

Foods and drink all becoming genetic
Electronic products on the rise
With someone getting rich, in disguise
Are we blind? Or, are we just pathetic

It's not to say, go back to how it was previously
It's not because I am growing old
It's because my soul hasn't been sold
We should use our faculties for humanity

Not sure if it's a pipedream, who can say
But, damn the oil that keeps spilling
Damn what we've done, all the killing
We all will pay for the bodies where they lay

Animals, woodland one by one the species fall
We're so deep in the hole, six feet below
Observations are clear as they go
Maybe it's just speculations, that's all

Guilty of Self-Interest

The verdict came down
The news is not good
Received to the day
Just like you knew it would

You struggle to face it
But what good would it do
You only seem to respond
When it applies to you

Then you look in your mirror
And what do you see
The person you worked on
So long and hard to be

Don't you like what you see?
Or, do you run from what you are?
The only problem with running away
Is how far

You face it with grace
And you take it in stride
Like the innocent charged
You've got nothing to hide

You step up to the stand
But have nothing to say
When the questions are over
You're taken away

The World I Live In

I live in a world of circles and stars
Of flying balloons, that travel to Mars

Inside I'm a rainbow, outside I'm a sin
I reach for the angels, but fall short again

I reason to wonder, I look to the past
Again falling under, memories that don't last

A room with a window, the snow falls on trees
With branches all glowing, I'm falling to my knees

What one asks for, it serves what one gets
To open the right door, to release our regrets

I live in my world, the world I create
Angel wings unfurl, surrounding me with fate

Talks with Yourself

Fortified will
Passionate subject to face
Agreed on solution
But, that's just not the case
So you walk out
Out into the landscape
Alone in all your solitude
Away from all the multitude
Change your tune and then your mood
Once again, in good shape
Back on track and in the groove
Spinning around and on the move
Take a bow, take off your shoes!
It's how you play the game, not win or lose
Pressure point pushed
Now it's anything goes
Deal out the cards
To your friends and your foes
Then, you walk out
Out into the sunlight
Alone with all your grand might
Left to fight the good fight
Soon, you start to feel right
No longer feeling uptight
Back on track and in the groove
Spinning around and on the move
Take a bow, take off your shoes
It's how you play the game, not win or lose

Stolid and true
Your conviction is sound
Emotionally speaking
Talks go round and round
So, you walk out
Out into the grey day
Far enough and far away
Maybe, for the whole day
Left to ponder anyway
What it was that made you stray
Now, back on track and in the groove
Spinning around and on the move
Take a bow, take off your shoes
It's the game of life, not win or lose

We Are Forgotten, Not Forsaken

We die by the life we forge
The stones we collect, wear us down
We march on like the ghosts of Valley Forge
Patriots of God are buried in the ground

Marble markers, scattered throughout
A humble caretaker rakes the grass
A sparkle of sunlight turns him about
Where our stone lies marked with an epitaph

Whatever we gathered, whatever we've loss
Will vanish in time with our name
Our cemetery marker will fade in moss
Hiding the stories of whence we came

Choices

Most of the time, they are good
We made all the life's choices we could
But, when did you last take a look?
Checkmate's at hand when the pawn beats the rook

Falling from grace, is the angel's fate
Never reaching the magic of Heaven's gate
How about you, will you choose right, and are you worth it?
Did you go through life honest, or did you fake it?

Old School Tough

A volatile nature he carries around
Two fists and knife can't put the man down
Let's see who's the victor?
To the victor, go the spoils
He'll turn up the heat till it reaches a boil

His fury will find you, no doubt about that
He'll blind you with punches at the drop of a hat
Let's see who is left standing
Let's see who will win
Once this god of thunder hits you on the chin

Severed by nature, abandoned in youth
Soon took to bars filled with gin and vermouth
Let's see you get by him
Go ahead, try and see
No second chance is his philosophy

His scars show disfigure, his gait is askew
With seldom a digit not blackened and blue
Let's see who is the richer
Let's see who is poor
No money will keep him from hitting some more

His fate is delivered he'll die by the gun
Like a fugitives justice he'll die on the run
Let's see if he runs now
When he faces a foe
With his deck full of aces, I'd say "no"

Hemlock

A stately tree, a hemlock
Spreading its branches like a peacock

Glorious in splendor to see
This coniferous life will outlive me

Thus, how could I not give it notice?
We encroached on it, it never chose us

I wonder if trees store memory energy
Will this living being I've met remember me?

I believe everyone should notice a tree
As they provide us with life giving gases constantly

As they help us, we should do as well
With this tree, I think I'll sit a spell

Another Made Soldier

Damn it soldier, kill!
Take the rising hill
Soldier boy, move your ass
Feel the bloody thrill

Crawl on to the top
Insane boy, never going to stop
Back and forth, projectiles fly
Each trigger pull goes "pop"

Slay the enemy
As far as you can see
Shattered bone and dripping blood
It's to be or not be

One by one on queue
Killer boy, this made you
Bayonet thrusts and gurgling sounds
Doing what you're trained to do

Help is on the way
Supposed to arrive today
Just one more kill, another life
Humble boy, starting to pray

No help either here or there
Nothing to trade, just futile despair
The enemy's coming for you, don't you know
Frightened boy, dying from fear

Ah . . .

Silence . . .

In a word, silence.
Disturbed, violence
Chaos madness, run
Crazy one with a gun

Solitude . . .

In a word, solitude
A peaceful interlude
Noise, crashing, loud
Lost yourself in a crowd

Meditate . . .

In a word, meditate
Mental image you create
Stress, fear, you can't stay still
Feed yourself a calming pill

Dreams . . .

In a word, dreams
It exist or it seems
Creeps that wake you
All the things you can't undo!

Revolution

Oppression forces concession
Dissention meets retaliation
Scandalous method of rule
Quash the loyalist consensus
Exact vengeance, no longer repress
A strike to the heart of convention
The charge with no means of egress
A ruse reveals the pretentions
Victory yields a newly formed order
Initially chaos is par for the course
Structured civility, leads to tranquility
The tyrannical foe reduced to woe
Ostracized by an ungovernable mass
Crush the opulent leaders that form
There pompous orgies offend
Odious men who conceal in their hollows
Oh, the misfortune and loathing that follows
Murderous hate disguised as a friend
Bloodlust, havoc, debauchery ensue
Moral decay and the rebellion again
Illusions, shattered start to disintegrate
A malformed society begins to self-destruct
Self-evident order truly put to the test
Thus dissolves, as followers reach the crest
Damn the oppressors, who bested the best

Seasons Change

It's clear that summer is over
The leaves changing, October
The bees have left the clover
Now is a time for reflection

Sun still breaks through the trees
Carrying a peaceful warm breeze
A mighty elm stands above me
This is a time to be thankful

A climbing squirrel goes about his way
Collecting food for a winter's day
A willow tree hangs in dismay
Life renewing will make us humble

Crickets chirp all around me
There hiding places, a mystery
Cotton clouds in the air, as far as I see
Remind us we are temporary here

The soil so fertile with its musty grain
Blades of grass, wet from yesterday's rain
A fortunate visitor of season, I am
I hope I can come back here again

We Are So Small

Look at the clouds, a glimpse of Heaven!
With the bread leaven, till full we eat
For the Lord has blessed us with Angel's and brethren
The teachers to guide us to a holy seat

Today, blue skies are filled with glory
One can interpret spirit in my prose and story
A sign showing mankind is good and enduring
We must hold hands and pray for wonders re-occurring

We can't look, but instead feel the power of the sun
A gift from the skies to warm us all
Just think how small we are to this mighty one
God need not lift a finger to make the sun fall

I praise and am humbled for my being here
Another day given to another unworthy one
The lord is forgiving to this soul, usually in despair
A chance to make good and wrong's undone

Superior

A large scraggly oak lies along her bushy grove
A fresh mist, splashes on the cove
Copper-rich cliffs line the lake
On the breakers and lighthouse, water breaks

It's summertime now and the sun is strong
On shore there are collector's colored stones all around
The water is frigid all the year long
Many a sailor has been lost to the her siren's song

Lake Superior in her vastness and grandeur
Thousands of iron ore laden ships have sailed here
A major waterway to haul ore and cargo
But from the surface, one can imagine ships lying below

The largest Great Lake shrouded in mystery and lore
Ghost ships, Specters have been reported before
God watch over sailors who venture out to sea
May you come home and the bell not ring for thee

Like the Edmund Fitzgerald, lost and famous, but only one
Of so many vessels vanished, that no longer run
Each frozen in time, all great ships as they go
She brings a frigid winter and lake effect snow

Seasons pass, but people will always remember
The twenty-nine tolls rang for men lost in November
When the waters churn and vicious winds blow
Brave men and their ships load up and for the Grace of God go.

Lake Superior is truly a wonder to behold
She shares her glory in the hot weather and the cold
Waters so clear for the honored dead and the living
She must be respected or she will not be forgiving

Caught in Ourselves

Forever caught in your existence
It's reasonable to plan resistance
But, best just take your life as it comes
Count the days and add up the sums
No good or bad just do what you feel
Sometimes the abstract life is more real
Don't live your life in a nautilus shell
Working your way out, building walls you dispel
Go forward to the light you can see
It's the forward thinker who reaches eternity

Just Thoughts

Why can life become so complicated?
Could it be that life is overrated?
We struggle, we search
We find things that hurt.
There's today, then tomorrow
And God knows what else
We remember yesterday
Like we really needed that
It's not like we can do anything about it
So, we fix, we work
We come home and tire
There are times when
Our relationships come down to the wire
There's pollution, encroachment
Spilled oil in the sea
I wouldn't want to be a tree, for sure
Our age of electronics and gadgets
Trees are a commodity
Dwindling along with space
Animals are dying and jungles trying
Trying to live, even people
Are being systematically killed
And someone on the front is lying
Like the hungry children
Like the propaganda on TV
Radio and newspapers, selling pain
While we waste away with acid rain
We are becoming robots
With computerized brains

No more Isaac Newton, no more Galileo
Math is solved on calculators
Thank goodness science has not yet killed faith
Or, maybe it has
And we haven't been told yet
People definitely don't have enough skills
Skills to communicate before someone kills
Where does someone like me fit in?
I speak with an accent, write with a prejudice
I listen to what I want to hear therein
Vehicles, Money too much green
Won't make it change only we can change
Government control and do what we're told
Soon a day with come when people will re-arrange
Maybe, the next hurricane, flood, tornado
Or, maybe when we're sold lies again we'll unfold
People can work together
But, someone needs to be in charge
Not the politicians who park fancy cars in their garage
Someone common, to give others direction
We have North, South, East and West
Looking towards the horizon, unsure of which is best
Maybe, this is some higher power's test

My Son at a Moment in Time

Running, just to avoid the grey
There it is, Coloring the day
Never stops, never goes away
Tired, breathing, going to fade

Going to fade to grey, unseen
All the running has made him lean
He's strong, agile, humble not mean
Made smart, a focused being

Has to keep running in order to be
Never tire, a wind blowing free
He's a thought you'll never see
He'll run himself into eternity

Then, he'll keep running
Running, till his end is coming.

Snow Storm

Snow, snow here we go! Here we go!
It's time to shovel. Shoveling snow!
Throwing white ice in the yard
Then, it's inside for hot cocoa

Another New England snow storm
To the locals, just the norm
It's reported five years since this much snow
Cotton white blanket from the big blow

Two feet thick, when measured right
Snowfall raining down since the night
Roads are empty, businesses close
Trees slump heavy, nearby ponds froze

Low temperatures climb slowly at best
This is a good day to stay in and rest
But, flakes still fall from heaven to below
So, that means time to shovel more snow!
Here we go! Here we go!

The Cardinals

Yesterday, the cardinals came
As I peered out the window
Flying about to and fro like a game
Stopping to feed on the thorny brush below

Perhaps a simple sight in December
As law of attraction brought them to me
In a smile, I hoped I would always remember
The wonderful life I have been given to see

Besides the white snow, colors grey and brown
The nature of winter trees, growing slowly, still
Squirrels leap from branches make a rustling sound
The woodland void of silence they fill

Other birds to visit, sparrows, a cedar waxwing
Senses acute each very alert as they feed
What a delight in a moment to my soul do they bring
For when their voices sing, then come the colors of Spring!

For a Butterfly, Days Fly

Butterfly, you carry too much beauty to name
You're a whimsical delight little flyer who came
Its noontime, I pray no bird finds his game
No matter, like your short life we all pass the same

When weather starts changing in late September
You don't visit as often as I can remember
Leaves take to flying in the wind's blow
Where do the flying bees go? I don't know

As the sun shines brightly, the sky turns to art
It's the early riser who sees the magic, smart
Tidbits of color still in the flowers that hold
Perennials however making plans for the cold

Today, from my vantage a huge willow tree
Scraggly limbs, weak and reaching for me
What fanciful moments before my eyes
But, today my eyes seek the last of the butterflies!

Crows

I saw a Murder of Crows
Fearless birds of black
Looking at me, me staring back
Smart I assume as birds go
Formidable force in a row

I continued past
As they took to the grass
Cunning, daring birds amass
As I walked, not a sound
Or, a flutter did resound

They took a defensive stance
Moving about as if in a dance
Searching for insects no doubt
Each purposely moving about

I considered it was time
For me to leave and bow out

It All Changed

Nothing is as it was then, not the same
As it was way back when
A simpler life was structured then
Small towns, hope no large powers to blame

The earth is surely changing
Making those of us who remember
That soon there'll be no resources
Eco-systems are all re-arranging

We have dying fish in the sea
Way too much use of military
What's happening isn't ordinary
Disasters occurring now regularly

Years ago, there wasn't so much worry
Everyone now is a germaphobe
Health is a problem throughout the globe
Now, in a time driven world we scurry

I know we all feel it, most people talk
The earth's crisis is surely rising
There's no more time for compromising
Our powerful leaders play dumb and balk

Maybe end days are coming real soon
The signs are there, just about everywhere
In the dirty air, on the ground crop circles
Not spaceships! Just some luny-toons

We're killing each other in far off places
It's not the first war, I remember many before
Our children goddamn it, are not worth dying for
In war, no one wins, but leaders think so, look in their faces

The religious war in the Middle East won't be the last one
There's an unseen message out there to end it
So, why does our country proudly extend it?

Simple Tree

Simple tree
Amazing tree!
I always see
As I drive by thee.

You grow there
Seemingly without care
While trucks and cars
Rush by, loudly

You are a birch tree
With other trees in the vicinity
Your white bark stands out
Right now, your leaves without

But, every season I can see
Your everlasting beauty
I've seen you yellow and green
With all the changes in-between

I wonder how many don't see you
Rushing by, too many things to do
Or, maybe many have looked; I don't know
Perhaps they too have watched you grow

Whatever your secrets are
I couldn't imagine by far
I could learn a lot from your wood
Truly, I myself could

I know you're not the only tree
But, that makes you no less special to me
If you weren't special, I'd just drive by
Not a glimpse of you would catch my eye

I wish to have your calm and strength
Not perfect, but stately with branches bent
Perhaps I do, that's a possibility
You are there to remind me of what I can't see

Yesterday, again I saw my special tree
My simple white birch, pleasing me
What was that . . . a cedar nearby?
I couldn't be sure as it caught my eye

For sure a coniferous tree
Or, a clump of them perceivably
Keeping my simple tree company
Just waiting for me to pass by and see!

Water

A bottle of water rests on the table
Within reach, I'm thirsty and able
So, without pause I lift it up
The pure liquid inside, I pour in my cup

With the cup to my mouth, I take a drink
As I swallow the refreshment I think
This is life's essence, the divine's gift for sure
It brings life like the sun, like a cure

It's worth more than gold, for gold can't save you
You can't live without it, even if you wanted to
We must not take its supplies for granted to ensure
The human race and all life will endure

Tree roots seek it, micro-organisms tweak it
It erodes the earth and forms land by the bit
It can render the largest mountains to grit
A powerful substance, no doubt about it

As soon as I drink it I feel its power
Like a drug I will seek it by the hour
I place my cup down and look at the bottle
"Thank you" I say as I press on in full throttle!

Love's Suicide

Folded, a message inside
When opened, she cried
Honesty was a must
He left her with broken trust
Who can she open up to?
Someone who went through it too?
Sadness, falling into a hole
Someone has ripped out her soul
Nothing left, empty and blue
The blackness she sees is true
Once, she was all glowing
All positive energy flowing
Now, a picture painted wrong
A musician who wrote her a sad song
With conviction, she starts to feel hate
In realization, she knows it's too late
So, distraught, she decides to be dead
She can't silence the noise in her head
She opens a window, looks deep at the ground
So peaceful now, she thinks, no sound
All's forgotten, going down

Bottom

A reduction in paycheck that won't pay the rent
A landlord who stingily won't budge a cent
Eviction is certain for this unfortunate man
His wife of ten years just up and ran

From predator he becomes the prey in the dark
On this unwanted journey he must now embark
Removed from the classes, he must now await
His journey to hell or his choice, heaven's gate

He tried to be common, he worked to be true
But, sad life reminds one of what can happen to you
One night seeking food he becomes a mark
He is found murdered near his old home, in the park

King'ers

A chestnut swung from a shoe-string
A chestnut broke, a rejoicing
A king is born in this game of chance
But, not the kind of knights and romance

A simple game made up by typical boys
Forgotten games created, like past toys
King'ers was a game passed down
The object, crush the opponents chestnut and win the crown!

Each collected precious chestnuts from nearby trees
Unfortunately, many a time we disturbed bees!
But, it was all worth it in the end
Just to have a chance to be winner again

The rules were simple, there was only one king
Others wore paper bracelets with chestnut, waiting
When the time came to challenge, you uncovered your hopeful winner
Of course, it was hard to claim winner as a beginner

One day, your turn came and it was game at hand
You had taken care of your chestnut to make your stand
Chestnuts were dipped in varnish and left to dry
A hole was nailed through the center, like an eye

A shoe-string was knotted and the chestnut slipped down
After careful consideration, it was time to get the crown
At first, your new chestnut was only worth "one"
Breaking others chestnuts increased your nuts value making it fun

Say one person had a chestnut that was valued at "four"
If you beat your opponent, then your "one" increased four more!
So, now you had a chestnut that was worth five
Gaining points, having the king challenge you, was the fun you derive

The day came when your chestnut was worth quite a bit
Now, the greedy king knew this and would have no part of it
The challenge was made, he singled you out
The king's champion chestnut and yours were taken out

Placed on their shoelaces, wrapping the lace around the hand
The lace was wrapped many times, so a good strike would land
The king would go first, you'd let your chestnut dangle down
The king's chestnut was battle fatigued, but this meant the crown

With a shoelace wrapped hand and the other for hold and aim
The king eyeing your chestnut's sway, aim and then the blow came
"Crack" was the sound as your chestnut swung around
But, it didn't break, not a split, just a "sigh of relief" sound

Now it was your turn at the king's prize and his woe
Readying yourself, you wrapped the shoelace tight to go
Your aim was true, your target clear, you delivered the blow
"Crack" was the sound as the king's prize chestnut, fell below

Silence befell over the fallen soldier, the war of the chestnuts ended
You'd won the throne, so the kings crown he surrendered
All the combined points of his champion passed on to you
Now, it was "your" throne all the challengers wished to undo

Life's Washing Machine

Spinning in cycles
Falling within
Shaking the body
It's time to begin

Solutions to add
Grime to dissolve
A costly reminder
Of dirt to resolve

To sit in a corner
To watch the inside
The heat fills a void
That we put aside

The many, the few
We all play the game
Some stand, some fall
In the end, we're the same

We must pay to keep going
Or, we'll stop and unwind
When the warm air stops blowing
There's a cold, so unkind

Tossing and turning
It may be out of control
The circular cycling
Is taking its toll

Time to Pay

End this charade!
Stop your parade
There's cost to be paid
Some bones to be laid

No encore to the show
Just empty places to go
Lost faces lying down low
Grave markers near, a stone's throw

Wroth-iron fence, black
Friend to the devil, Jack
Hoof-prints found on a track
Lead to memories kept in a sack

The crescent moon's dim light
Glows moss green and shadows bright
Something's come to make thing right
Souls will be sowed tonight

Too Much

Errands to run
Too many places
Too many people
Humid, hot sun

Complete, must come
Too much to take
Too hard to think
Too difficult a sum

The sum of what you are
Too many memories
Too many lost years
Always, near, but too far

Surreal your existence
Too many changes
Too fast for angels
Too tired for resistance

So much uselessness to do
Too much to fathom
Too many rules
The whole world, then you . . .
And you haven't got a clue

A Notion

There, I stood on a snow-covered hill, in a quiet winter's world
For a moment, just one moment, I felt like I'd been crowned king
Just like a flag rising on a stationary pole, my soul was lifted and unfurled
I was alive, God so much alive that I let my spirit rise and sing!

As I stood silent for that one moment in peace, I smiled and closed my eyes
Then, just for another moment, I had a notion and
thanked my God for giving me life.
Though, I knew that this moment of solitude wasn't meant to survive
That with this ultimate calmness in life,
comes the balance of daily struggles and strife

So, I opened my eyes and walked down from my hill,
leaving that place of peace
I walked back to the world we face every day,
one of machines and motion
Back to the schedules and deadlines and expectations,
a hurried world of unease
But . . . serenity now lay within me,
a peaceful place in the form of a notion

Found Body

Spiraling up
Spiraling down
Standing vertical
Horizontal ground
Stink in water and float
Drowned, putrid bloat
Found near shore
Carcass of gore
Graying blue
Sickening view
Nothing new
Found by you
Pile of shit
A human deposit
Who to tell?
You knew this person well
You'd be suspect one
Under the gun
Got to be
The one who didn't see
Act like nothing's wrong
Moving sideways
Hey, not your problem anyways

Rain

Raindrops fall
Pitter-patter
Cloud-born matter
Puddles, they splatter
Softly, steadily, soothing
A cool breeze ushers in
The warm summer night
No moon in sight
Just dark and streetlight
A soft glow, below, my window
Trees like ghosts stand
Ghosts I can see
However barely
Still, but noticeably
They whisper, they shadow their past
Rain comes for cooling
Summer's heat
A quiet street
Sidewalks of concrete
All shining anew, cleansed, renewed
A peace so intense
Quiet is almost a sound
Audible all around
From heaven to the ground
Balance is happening, right now
Such a special time
Noticeable to me, tonight
Everything I see, just right
Tonight, rain brings delight
For it is life giving matter
Going pitter-patter

Are we imagined?

Watching the movies
Like life they surprise
We see what's not real
Unfold before our eyes

We read then, we wonder
Our thoughts run away
We dream of our visions
As we pass the time away

Subconsciously we seem
To be living in a dream
Are we just unaware?
Of our unconscious fare

Looking at photos
We reminisce of a time
When days seemed simpler
When the rhythm had rhyme

Like a movie our life is set
We fill our days with action
Some remembered, some we forget
We're a picture not taken yet

So, we watch another movie
It's us on the screen
We're acting out ourselves
In a movie fairytale scene

Not real, but imagined
Sort of like the real thing
Did we only imagine ourselves?
From the very beginning

Someone Lost

A simple psalm of silence
A reason to believe
I lost you and I'm sorry
There must be time to grieve

The passing of time brings change
There are moments I feel so lost
It only takes one moment to age
I will find you, no matter the cost

I wake up and find myself weeping
With hope I will get through the day
The memories of you are seeping
Into darkness you are fading away

Each day I must deal with the guilt
After guilt, I deal with the shame
Somehow, I lost everything we built
Left a hole in my soul and my name

Someone said "things happen for a reason"
This seems to ease the questions why
But, I doubt that fate is what to believe in
We can fill our souls before we die

I wonder where you are out there
I wonder what tomorrow may bring
Believe me, I will search everywhere
Till I bring you home in my heart again

My Winged Friend

The softest sound I heard
From the tinniest prettiest bird
Very close, in a sparsely branched tree
I could hear her ticking at me
A little brown bird with russet-topped head
Perhaps, asking me to be fed
My heart glowed to the core
As she followed me to trees, four
I tried to mimic her call
A simple chirp was all
I couldn't believe what I was seeing!
A gift of nature so very freeing
How to know she was female, I assumed
She was of lesser color, plumed
We had communicated for sure
How? Was a mystery, obscure
As I smiled and humbly walked away
My little friend still wanted to play
Fluttering, she eventually flew into space
For me, something incredible took place
A wonderful passing gift for me
My little winged friend speaking, seemingly

Tea

A cup of brewed tea, simplicity
Offered to guests complimentary
Tea for me lately
Has become a daily treat!

To sit, to sip, to ponder
A peaceful mind goes to wonder
Comfortable chair in the sun
Just enough shade to cool one

At ease in a resplendent place
The many flavors put a smile on my face
No tension, not a single trace
Just a cup, saucer and a bit of old-fashioned grace, tea.

Keep Your Heart Warm

It melts during the day
Then, it freezes at night
A snow-cold heart
Melts blood in the sunlight

When the heart grows hard
It can't bleed at all
Feelings just die
Then, the joys of life just fall

True, days and nights will flow
A moon rises a yellowish white
The sunlight surprises
A star that conquers the night

Sleep on the moon, but wake in the sun
Live in joy and light, not dark and vain
We are all children of a chosen one
That cleanses souls with intermittent rain

Withered One

Tired
Of all that transpired
Confused
By the game of win or lose
Battered
From all that matters
Falling
I find myself crawling
Slowly
I merge in with the lonely
Sadly
My life becomes madly
Broken
Before I was even awoken
Trying
To keep my soul from frying
Finally
In a quiet grave, I'm lying

Post-Traumatic Stress Disorder (PTSD)

There's a fear in me
The kind that an open mind
Doesn't want to see

So, inside I suppress in my head
My dread won't give in
To an openness

To open means
Having to face "the one"
The self-identity on the run

Inside myself I crawl
The reasons for it all
Is revealed in my crystal ball

Am I a monster or a beast?
Can I take the responsibility?
Or, use a little white lie, insecurity

I know this for sure
As God as my keeper, I don't want more
I want to unlock my psychological door

My biggest fear is "me"
A "me" my eyes don't wish to see
But, until I look, I won't be free

The Circus-Carnival

Congratulations Mr. Jones, on your
Never ending, mind-bending consternation
As you make your final preparation
For your first-ever indoctrination
Into our "by reservation only" tour

Now, don't you hesitate, go, go, and go
Or worse yet my friend, procrastinate
Much worse, god forbid you'd be late
And unfortunately miss the last gate
Of the train to the circus show

Colored streamers and clowns, there
Women in petticoat gowns
Pole tents built in the round
Confetti covering the ground
Smells of apples and popcorn in the air

A wonderful fun-filled place to go
Lights that shine like the sun
Pop a balloon with a BB-gun
Watch the lions and tigers run
As acrobats fly above the circle below

Get your fortune read for just a dime
Throw a ball through a hoop
Stop by a stand for an ice-cream scoop
Take a ride in a roller-coaster loop
Enter a house of mystery and stop time

Get scared in the castle of fright
Toss a bean bag for tic-tac-toe
Pick a number and spin the wheel slow
Make a rubber banana boat go
Just a bit, really for the entire night

Just sign here and you're invited
Fear not for taking a chance, sir
With luck, you'll meet a beautiful dancer
Or, a three-eyed female necromancer
We just know that you'll be delighted!

We Fade Like Pictures

Flashing shadows whisper
In the land of mirrors
Peering through the haze
Of, a blurred silver glass

Speaking your mind softly
So, others will listen
To them, hearing words brush
Lives of their very beings

Now the bright green holly
Wears the signs of snow
Ushers the days forgotten
Winds of woe so often blow

We build walls of ages
Zones of time we create
Hiding our fears and frailties
Soon we become pictures to be lost

With certainty death is alive
Feeding on our wailing memories
If we become blind we might hear
The fortunate life of yesteryear

Tried as I Might

I stared to shout and scream and pout when I saw your face
It was just a mistake, a fib, a lie, to me a final disgrace
Then in one second's flash, a flick, a dash, I made a mess of your space
I decided to run, to leave to go to some other place

Then came lights, the sights, the sounds, as I looked back to you
It was all I could take, forsake, partake, in the best thing to do
So, I decided to fly, to try, to jump from the bridge over blue
As I started to fall, to dream, to fly into the widening view

Along came the black, the blue, the lack of what's left of me
In a moment of haste, of clear, of waste it was all I could be
That's when you sang your song, so wrong, so blind that no one could see
You were all you could be, become, deceive, those around you who believe

It's the chain of events
That makes us each
Reach for the moments
Just seemingly out of reach

It's all in a grain of wheat
We eat to grow strong
That makes us feel complete
To feel as though we belong

Like a chain with a ball
That keeps each of us down
In a life surrounding us all
Till we return to the ground

Tried as I might
Finished, tried and true
Time to give up the fight
I walked right out on cue

The Day I Discovered I was dead

October 21st, I walk in the park
I'm dead
People don't notice me
Like a mist they can't see
Moving, settling, too obscure
I'm lonely I'm confused and not sure
What it is about me, others ignore?
It's like I said before
I'm dead
I drift in my own way, alone today
Maybe it was always this way?
My book of self was thrown away
Long ago my mind went astray
My journey some used to say
Can some force reroute me?
Intercede in a way that will light me?
I'm sure, I know I'm here
But, shunned to not interfere
I must be dead
The park is just a "there"
The lifeless form wanting somewhere
Did I drift too far to be in repair?
Is it possible for the dead to smell the air?
I walk by a woman and a child in a chair
I smile with emotions, sincere
But they don't react, going on with no care
I have to be dead
Where did my exuberance go?
I used to have enchantment and zeal
I'm my own enemy when I try to expose
The man I once was, now in repose
I surrender myself, unapparent and morose
For, I am dead

Pardon Me

Pardon me for lying
Pardon me for dying
Inside is gone
An empty shell
Pardon me for trying

Pardon me, when you see me
Broken trust, liability
Flooded with doubt
A king without
Pardon my liberty

A brightness that burns
The horizon grows black
A candle that melts
Lying here, wishing you back

Pardon my emotion
Pardon my conviction
Said to this man
Can't flee if you can
You're moving in slow motion

A brightness that yearns
With dishonor comes black
I'm a candle that burned
Dying here wanting you back

Facing Hate

When you face hate
How can you be kind?
Hate may forever gyrate
On a string you can't unwind

Dead emotions start to smell
Soon, rotting they spread
The innocent can see and tell
The string now just a fraying thread

No good can come out
From one hiding hate inside
What is kept silent is a shout
Of condescending pride

Too much pride can scar
Like iron that turns to rust
Too deep to rescue, too far
How deep the scar of trust?

I know one who hates with grudge
Cold-hearted train of thought
Irrational blame, won't budge
No temperate disposition being sought

So, how do you stare at hate's face?
How do you take the unfair?
Most would cut ties, not a trace
Chided, bullheaded and gored from the rear

I maintain my hold for now
But, if nothing changes I'll stop contact
I may feel regretful somehow
But, how many times can you face attack?

Does the Present Exist?

Why does the future haunt me?
Gone is the past, but I can't let go

Thus, stuck in the present, its in-between
Dimensions of living that can't be seen

I look for an answer, but it's not there
A traveler of life, not a moment to spare

When I look back and see how far memories go
The mind is a camera with its pictures to show

Motion is constant, does the present exist?
Future takes over present, it can't resist

We should live in the present, so others say
Save the future to unfold another day

So what is the game, where are we now
Are we past, present or future somehow

Maybe the truth is that we are all three
It changes from one to the other we can't see

Doomsday

Your favorite time of year is here
The leaves are falling everywhere
See them fall

It's just another year to you
You think that you've made it through
Think again

Something has gone wrong this year
There are people dying everywhere
Can't you see it?
Can't you feel it?
Don't you know?

That, Doomsday is finally here
Something called Death has filled the air
It's over just sitting and waiting to die
Your turn will sooner pass you by

Don't you hear the thunder everywhere?
Can't you see the darkness in the air?
Don't you know there's nothing you can do?
But, pray to God you'll make it through

Feeling like you want to cry
Not a tear will fill your eye
You know why

People are all running scared
The day is here, the one they feared
For so long

But no one seems to understand
No one wanted to lend a human hand
Can't you see it?
Can't you feel it?
Didn't we know?

Eternal Battle

Devil, Devil in the night
Watching, spreads his wings and takes flight
An Angel wears a veil of light
Watching, steers you to the right

They forced a man upon a hill
Ripped him so his blood would spill
Crossed him with a rage to kill
The will of God had been fulfilled

Devil, Revels in delight
Planning the ways to man's demise
Angel waits ready for the fight
Knowing, soon the Christ will rise

It's up to us
We have a choice
We can be God's voice

The Third Knight

The first knight died in glory
The second knight died in vain
The third knight lived to tell the story
As the charge surged, he chose to abstain

When the thousands crashed into each other
It's the heroes in front who fell down
By sword, they killed one another
For their king with the golden crown

Alas, now the dead are too many to count
As barrels of blood seep into the soil
The king only flinches, as he saddles his mount
A victor of sorts, of this bloody turmoil

His soldiers walk amongst the field
Killing enemy wounded with a thrust of a spear
No matter if the enemy chooses to yield
No mercy will be afforded to the dying here

The third knight, who stayed back at the attack
From rushing in the thunderous crash
Has been paid with a gold-filled sack
Whilst his brethren now lie in a ground of ash

For, it was the third knight who chose wisely
He lives, not as a coward, but alive and well
His shrewdness applied at a time so precisely
Has afforded him heaven's life, not a butcher's hell

Reaction

I lean against a post
It breaks
I walk on the earth
It shakes
I feel my heart
It stills
I feel my love loss
It kills
I stand in a river
It flows
I drop a seed
It grows
I am flustered
It shows
I fear the lion
It knows
I talk to a dog
It listens
I place glass in the sunlight
It glistens
I open a letter
It rips
I toss a coin
It flips
I twist a cap
It frees
I hear a lie
It deceives
I see the truth
It releases
I feel understood
It eases
This poem is an idea
It conceives

Lost in Myself

So many paths appear, I can't debate
So many faces pass also, so I stand in place
I'm here to find my own human race
Beyond my fringe of madness for madness sake

The memories seem too far away
Too far for me to reach, I need a break
A twisted man in an endless maze
I find my way and my journey is safe

But, can I find my way back, where I was there?
Can I fill missing parts that I lack here?
I'm lost and need to find my way back home
In my state of mind, best not to face the world alone

The tides of the ocean don't stop, they sound
The spirit of time keeps moving like a clock going around
I once was hero of my time, with no request for reward
My fate, a king who will die by own his sword

Problems

I'm perplexed, hexed
It's one dilemma after the next
I'm a witch whose mark is vexed
How to make you construe?
How do I put it all together and tell you?
Since, you have your own point of view
It's likely that what I say won't do
My own restlessness is growing
I've an indication of where this is going
Unfortunately, I find no peace in knowing
I'm resolute as they say "hanging in there"
But, in my mystification, there's disrepair
Being tired of the emptiness and puzzles here
It's time to renew, revitalize and set right
Grow my own wings and take flight
Yeah, a refugee who vanished in the night!

Dreary Day

It's raining today
Bleak I must say
Gray and grim
The lighting, dim
Inside there's light
But, not too bright
Not like sunlight
That's just right
This makes you tire
Lose your desire
I'm feeling blue
Nothing I can do
I could write?
Yes, here I delight
So, I ensue
But, words are few
It's raining hard
I see in the yard
Puddles forming
Skies storming
In a window I gape
For a chance to escape
Will I go?
I don't know
I'm feeling lazy
A bit stir crazy
Crazy to stay
Inside for the day
Well, hey
That's perfectly o.k.

Words Don't Let Go

You tried, but left to no recourse
You're soaking in your own remorse
Sad sometimes what people do
In the end, you're left with you
Reasons aren't on the menu
Understanding doesn't serve you
Alone in your own demise
Fighting a final reprise
Seeking substances to make you feel
A dream unfolds, but isn't real
The mistake comes when you reveal
The bitch of you having to deal
Deal with what you feel is real
To make your peace and concede
On to other matters, slowly or, quick
Reflect the thoughts that made you sick
Seek the easy, passive, slow and legit
Take your mind and make a go of it
But, words remain, remind, you know
We let go of words, but words don't let go

Choosing Alone

An effect of the society around me
Has caused me to be all alone
Society and the fact that my voice
Doesn't seem to carry the right tone

Who would hear me and understand
Who would listen to stories I tell
Can you answer and be realistic
Because lies will drive you to hell

Everyone's busy with themselves
No one wants to listen to you, it's true
Because keeping up with the one
They don't have time for two

Alone will probably drive me insane
A small problem I have to toil with
Maybe this will eventually kill me
But, then I don't have to die, bit by bit

Society, family, friends, try to own you
At times there's nothing to believe in
Seems the only way I can fit in
Is to find my little alone space within

When I want to know what's what
Drugs help me to reach an even keel
Watch from alternate dimensions
To escape reality, hide from what's real

Still, I have to keep up with crazy life
My guess is, I'll be staying on my own
Smartly keeping up with the social duties
My guess is that . . . I'll stay alone.

A Drive

A drive on the way back home
On a desolate road, somewhat unknown
Through a desert landscaped zone
Behind the cars wheel, you're all alone

The radio songs sing loud and strong
Blue skies fading purple as you move along
Just the headlights to guide your way
Through darkening hours, that end the day

You're on your way to freedom now
It lies just beyond your reach somehow
As you press the cars pedal down
To pass another empty quiet town

In the dark now, you begin to see
Just ahead lies who you want to be
You question if anyone's ever truly free
Or, is where you are, who you're meant to be?

Endless turns, revealing endless skies
As the starlit blackness fills your eyes
Roadway markings that guide your way
From the life you chose to live today

Look ahead! There lies your tomorrow
No need to ask, beg steal or borrow
Just decide on who you want to be
When day breaks, you will once again see

That the road you are on is called fate
One thing to remember is it's never too late
To change your direction as you drive along
Your choice, no such thing as right or wrong

Broken Hearted Song

A singer wants to sing his song
He hopes the words will come along
So, he starts to put the words to pen
Then, tries to find the notes to send

With just his feeble voice, he starts
Like a lost soul pouring out his heart
In hopes of righting something wrong
No words to make right, only a song

Mary, what do I say?
To take this pain away
Sorry, that I lost you
For all the hurt I caused you

Mary, what can I do?
To make it up to you
A simple man with a simple song
I've loved you for so long

Mary, where are you now?
May my song reach you somehow
I think of you now, all day long
Just can't stop singing your song

As the singer sings, his notes off-key
He becomes as free as his melody
Guitar strings strumming his song you see
As the singer's notes ring, then suddenly

His heart opens wide, as wide as a door
Sound waves shake at his inner core
With each breath he feels like never before
As his guitar bellows, there's pain no more

Mary, what do I say?
To take your pain away
Sorry that I lost you
For all the hurt I caused, too

Mary please don't cry
As I sing you my lullaby
Dry the tears from your eye
Lift your spirit high in the sky

Mary, what can I do?
To make it up to you
This simple man, with nothing more
I give you my song, forevermore

Loss and Rejection

The pain of loss and rejection are like no other
My first wife's rejection and the death of my brother
Everything changed when dad passed in 2007
My nerves broke down when my new wife left in 2011

I suffer anxiety of the "come what may"
Gather myself up and put on my show today
One thing I've learned is no one want's your fear
Not that they don't acknowledge you, or care

Everyone is a soul that takes care of its own
We each have a note that sounds its unique tone
Waves of music mixing all in a chord
People comfort, but your troubles they can't afford

I've no idea what chapter of life I'm in
Or, how many pages before the next one begins
I'm a husband, a father and not without sin
So, I pray to my god to make me smile again

The Best of Being

I can see so clear from here
My home
A home that is everywhere
For I am a resonating being
Connected to all things
The clarity I'm seeing, is freeing
An open mind
Keep the beautiful from fleeting
No good is lost
I'm a positive force repeating
I'm a clean river flowing
Around ancient stones
Sprinkled with fireflies glowing
The light reflection allows me to see
A mighty earth
Towering above in her majesty
Open sky, only shooting stars can fall
Tonight
The meteorites are best of all
To be savored for another night
So to share
With another, wish of delight
I sense my aura, a cool blue
At peace
With a love of all things, so true
If one moment our world could feel
A passive quiet joy
I believe by grace all things would heal

Grandfather Old Man (Pour Mon Pepe)

Grandfather old man, where did you go?
You taught me the truth and all that I know
Except life's imperfections I learned on my own
Can you hear me and see me, now that I've grown?

Grandfather old man what's on your mind?
The more I wonder the more that I find
Good advice for the taking that you left behind
Can you touch me; tell me if my life's on the line?

Grandfather, Grandpa, there till the end
More than a mentor, you were my friend
But, your memories are fading and time seems to fly
Can you reach me to teach me what it's like to die?

Grandfather old man, would you know
Those times are changing and days seem to go
But, the lessons you taught me move purposely slow
I seek you, the thank you for the many things I have to sow

Tu est mon coeur Pepe

Wonderful Daylight

Daylight hurry, come quickly!
Light the day bright
Oh, wondrous event such a wonderful sight!

How would it be?
If we could not see
Beyond the dark of night
With light doth comes such a delight!

For me, I sit . . .
And bit by bit
The daylight's fire is slowly lit
With sunlight comes life, I praise it.

No longer is it dark
And hark, what was that sound?
Behind the leaves and tree bark
Beautiful sound of the meadowlark

Daylight doesn't come quickly enough for me!

All in Time

Now you're gone
Far from home

I never believed you
I thought you deceived me
The little I listened
To lies, that you fed me

On you own
Place unknown

It's just what you wanted
You left without warning
Not once did you waiver
You waited till morning

Truths be known
Trouble prone

It's what you intended
Your plan had unfolded
The silence you shouted
The night you were scolded

Growing old
Left alone

A conscience will guide you
Your heart may divide you
Love's door will be open
Should your soul decide to

Coming home
Wrongs atoned

For whatever the reasons
I'm the sorry one
It was never my intention
To make you want to run

Hurts to repair
Emotional care

If only we could take back time
Just a day, alone
Is all the love we'd need to help us both
Find our way home

Beautiful Women

Pretty women make me shy
At times, it's hard to look them in the eye
My esteem may be low, I don't know
I always wonder what the girls see
When they smile and look at me
Do they acknowledge my presence?
Can they sense and smell my essence?
Do they see bald, short or old?
Do they seek the tall, dark and bold?
For me, I approach pretty women gently
I'm cordial but never a "catch" evidently
In this age, seems pretty women abound
Even very young women dress to kill
Seductive temptations render a heart still
Beautiful women can reduce you at will
A flashing neck, toss of hair weakens the will
Pretty women like nature are full of wonder
Gentle like wind and strong like thunder
Curvaceous, full-figured, thin and tall
Long-legged, long, short hair, I love them all!
Dark hair, dark eyes, blond with blue eyes
Colored hair, green eyes, freckles mesmerize
Wherever I go, I see women that are pretty
The country, the beach, park and the city
In malls, beauties gather around
Not one spot where beauties don't abound
Yes eyeing beautiful women brings me glee
So, for the rest of my life I'll be happy!

Childhood Magic

Magical shadows cast
Under thick barked shady trees
Brings about reflections of childhood
A secret place of comfort, once visited

Glimmering rainbows sparkle
On a wind-swept lakes surface
Dancing fairies of thought, once believed in
That anything, everything, is possible

Winter's icy silent solitude
Shows a star-speckled heaven
Spreading infinite blessings of mortality
Opening the mind's eye to individuality, pondered

Floating leaves swirl in a cyclone of wind
Displaying their magnificent colors
Remind us of days past and a cycle of life
Where dreams of possibility seem endless

My Best Friend (For Kazoo)

The best friend in my life
Is a dog, not my wife
Why? Because people bring strife
With my dog, only loving good life

There's no man luckier than me
I found God in my dog, truly
He brings me peace, love and joy
When I come home, he's like a little boy

Happy and faithful and glad I'm there
When I greet him, I don't have a care
Don't get me wrong, I love my girl
She's the best love in the world

But, my dog, he's something more
Like a great show, he's the encore
The part where you wish, it would never end
When you'd give all to see it again

That's my friend, my dog "Kazoo"
To my death, to my dog I'll remain true
I know, I saw he'd do the same for me
I'll carry Kazoo in my heart for eternity

I love you Kazoo
Please don't be offended my wife, I love you too.
It's a different love, that's all
It's a love that can not fall, ever at all

Abuse (For Melissa)

She said "I'd love you daddy," if I could just break up
All the anger you scarred me with, when I was growing up
You see, my life's so empty I can hardly feel
Seems I don't know what's right or when it's real

But daddy, it's time for me now, time for me
There's a lifetime inside, I want you to see
I'm a candle of light, that's always burning bright
Burning endlessly, from now into the eternal night

All the pain and suffering you put me through
Left a path of rejection, that leads to you
I'm grown up now, so many things I know
How a seed not watered well, will never grow

Hey, I'm still myself, when I look I see a flower
I'm a cool wind, a passion fruit that will never sour
Look at me daddy I'm the little house that's red
I'm the little girl of wonder, in the children's book I read

In order to know me, then you'll have to heal and forgive
Heal the wounds you created when you made me live
Or, when your well dries up and it's time for you to go
You'll leave a little girl inside your heart, you didn't know

Sometimes

Sometimes, I look over and feel you beside me
Like a light shining that opens my eyes
A brilliant new day, just like no other place
A wonderful feeling puts a smile on my face

Sometimes, I reach over and feel you inside me
Like the embers that give the fire its glow
All warm-hearted scents, such a memorable place
A comfort like no other puts a smile on my face

Sometimes, I think back and feel you around me
Like the air that I breathe, that keeps me alive
A breeze that surrounds me, I feel your embrace
Of the gentle winds brush, that puts a smile on my face

Until

Can I be the only one who remembers?
The special moments our souls spent together
Am I the only one who thinks it does matter?
Enough to send my own words in a letter

I hope you can read my message of love
Because as it goes, it goes out solely to you
In hopes of opening the door to your heart
Allowing me through the distance that keeps us apart

I've fully committed and given myself to you
In every possible form, shape, matter and way
To deny me this truth I believe would be wrong
My one love and best friend I've known for so long

Sometimes the cloudiest, thickest haze in our lives
Can be so dense it's hard for us to see through
It requires a keen sense and sight to find our way
Always, that's when our love has brightened the day

We've always been there to help guide each other
No matter how difficult and trying the path has been
I've been the sailing ship and you've been my compass
Together we've navigated through the pass, just us

I'm sitting adrift now, on the same stormy sea
Keeping my God's faith that we'll find our path
Destination, towards your heart and soul my dearest friend
Churning waves on a course that I hope will never end

If I not reach the shore before life's sun sets
I'll moor not to my sadness and hoist up my sails
The winds, I'll let carry me towards your precious face
Until I reach you again my true love in another time and place

Until, I sit adrift in my sea of despair

Playing the Part

A torrid affair leaves love sadly behind
Now, just torment and rage and a life so unkind
Sleepless nights spent dancing awake in love's dreams
Just a foolish heart seeking remorse, as it seems

But, there's no pill to stop never-ending pain
Forever letting go, it keeps coming back again
Waking moments that jar the mind's conscious awake
Bring a prose of emotions only angels could make

For no mortal knows why certain events unfold
Thus, we ponder and philosophize, as we grow old
To make reason of queries we are not meant to know
We're just actors in audition for God's greatest show

A Lie Costs

Think it through
Think it through
Don't deny if it's true
It's easy to do
If it acquits you
A lie can never undo
Once a lie is spun
You start to become undone
It's like being on the run
As more lies spill, one by one
A fugitive from everyone
To lie is not to have won
So, take a minute
Sit and figure it
Time for grimace and grit
Again, it's easy to get by it
When you don't have to commit
So, think it through
The monster will always eat at you
With hope that liars remain few
Start by being upfront and true
Take in what's coming to you
Many will admire you
One good deed creates two

Beyond Feeling

So solemnly silent I sit here
Wounded heart in despair
Bleeding from the inside
For a love that has died

Great hurt beyond pain
Without hope I remain
Confusion reigns king
Today, no birds will sing

No song will be heard
Quiet and unspoken word
Thoughts running amuck
Mirror reflection of bad luck

So grey outside you can see
A wandering man that's me
Looking for love once had
Lines on his face spell sad

Unfortunately, driven mad
By true love sadly gone bad
Time now hunts the man
Remember him if you can

A light that shines no more
Object lost on the ocean floor
Worthy of endless search indeed
A needy heart continues to bleed

Not visible from the outside
Not due to caring true and tried
A forgotten lore remembered
Held beliefs finally surrendered

Deep In My Blue

The one I could always come to
The only one who I could run to
As you're no longer there
I'll be lost in despair
Deep in my blue

A hero in my life "I once knew"
The image I chose to look up to
I'm lost without you out there
With only a prayer
Deep in my blue

For answers I always turned to you
You taught me how to stay true
What it means to care
I hold you dear
Deep in my blue

You taught me it matters what we do
Now, I believe dreams do come true
You left stories to share
A breath of fresh air
Deep in my blue

If you hear me then hear "I miss you"
Tomorrow, I'll wake up without you
Not a moment I'll spare
Keep your memory near
Deep in my blue

So, I'll walk on alone as you'd do
I'll always remember to thank you
For giving your lessons so rare
Now, I can tackle my fear
Deep in my blue

Hyper-Vigilant

It helps when I let go
Of everything I know
Refreshing, enlightening
Open, but also frightening

I'm a target for some to kill
I'm an empty vessel to fill
Fill with hurt and lies
Led to a place where everything dies

Still, it helps when I close my eyes
Envision the earth and skies
It's so beautiful when I see
A place God made of eternity

No television, paper or radio
No pressure, nowhere to go
No propaganda and no place to hide
No need to fear being alive

I can be scary, but extremely nice
I wish I didn't have to think twice
It's evil that won't let me be
Always sucking me back to humanity

The Starlings

Five starlings perched on a fence
Perhaps they represent the five elements
Wind, earth, fire, ethereal and air
A reminder to me, we all come from there

As I watch the little birds dance
I fall into sort of a trance
There, five lives fluttering so clean
I wonder, what does all this mean?

Just a natural design or a grandiose purpose?
Something inside me began to surface
Life is so beautiful, the magic and wonder
We well believe, or we fall asunder

This very minute, my message was clear
Trust in a higher power, revel and revere
A prime number, sacred to my life here
Just five little mysteries I so endear

Holly Anne

Beautiful wonderful Holly Anne
You come to me from some fairytale land
So much yet for me to understand
Like how you magically make my life grand

Special woman who means everything to me
You carry unconditional love that sets me free
There are so many things I want to say
Like how you phone calls make my day

To express how I feel when I'm with you
Tis' simply just too difficult to do
That I love you, this much I know
My feelings will constantly show and grow

Holly Anne, "may I have this dance my dear?"
On our dance floor of life, if only you'll share
The slow dance of forever love, oh so rare
Spinning timeless in joy without a care

Intense, passionate love of my life
May I wish that someday, you'll be my wife?
That somewhere beneath the sun or the moon
Our love will consummate not late, but soon

Damn the Hope

Damn the hope that won't recede in me
Strike the heart that leaves me in pain
Left to figure it out by myself again

Why did I deserve such awful results?
I've never asked for this emotional assault
Nothing matters anymore and my life is at a halt

Colors are dull and plants have no leaves
Grasses are brown and the earth has no trees
Rocks are cold to touch and give no release

The clear sky represents the emptiness I feel
A huge vastness that dwells within my chest
Damn the hope what won't recede and damn the rest

Look Closely, Don't Dismiss

That which you would consider as inconsequential
Should be examined with utmost scrutiny
For it is there, that the enigma may be solved
In the overlooked, where the solution may lie

Never a test completed should have gone to waste
And no time allotted should be considered fruitless
Less the general opinion waiver to change such claim
Or, much doubt should arise to give one question

Beyond understanding lies truth yet undiscovered
Just behind the veil lies the means to the way
Yet, few who would venture by faith alone find
A brilliant conclusion for mankind, by such method

So, let us consider for a moment that perhaps
Intuition is the key to unlocking the door of mysticism
Act when presumption is given with clarity, or not
And believe in the outcome as the best possible result

Let it be then, what may be spiritual intervention
Or, perhaps just a number chosen at random, correct
Or, perhaps vibrating atoms are configured in a way
That their resonating motions, creates an illusion of sorts.

When My Dad Died

When my Dad died
I lost something inside
Starting my journey
To a personal suicide

Ripped me in half
Not so easy to laugh
Now I had changed
I felt the estranged

Boys, I was the last
Never knew, never asked
Haunting me with the past
Paper pictures don't last

What was carved in stone
Was the man who'd left me, alone
Who'd of known it was like this
I had made God's list

The list of who lives
Who goes on and gives
To take care of things
While an angel sings

When Dad left, he was blind
An act I felt was unkind
But, when I talked to Dad
He could envision what he'd had

The places he loved most
Father, Son and the Holy Ghost
There was a message there
For me to feel and hear

While the Father had gone
The son, I would carry on
With the help of the Holy Ghost
Whom now I rely on the most

The Red

Outside my window, I see red
Is the red outside, or in my head?
Fall, as colored leaves shed
Images of fallen me instead
Beautiful leaves of bloodshed
Military persons, the bodies fall
Move, move soldiers, face the call
Lives of honor who risk it all
Blood on the leaves, we can't see
Blood of the Father, son and our lady
Enemies taunt us, we go for more
A knock and we stupidly open the door
For more red blood spills on the ground
In America, life goes on, not a sound
The sound of a soldier dispensing a round
Another bloody body under a dirt mound
All the killing and blood make me vomit
When it all ends, nothing will come of it
I served in the Air Force for 20 years
I served overseas for half my career
I supported our conflicts while over there
When I returned home, no one seemed to care
When I mentioned the war, they look in the air
They just don't want to hear or see
The way of the military, disciplined misery
The Veteran's support each other
Like a family unit we call ourselves brother
Though we each served in our own way

There's a bond of experience, it won't go away
We all see red, some awake some asleep
The river of blood runs mind-deep
Like the red leaves that curtain the tree
There's blood on leaves and within me.

(Red leaves, red blood, our dead soldiers in the mud)

Demon Wants To Play

Cloudy little demon
Dancing with the moon
Don't you worry?
I'll be home soon
Then, you can dance
With me instead
After all, you little shit
You're already in my head
My imaginary clown
Spins a wheel of misery
Round and round and round
Making all senses dizzy
One little matter
That is very clear
Simple, I'm mentally not here
I'm out running a race
Finish line, my disgrace
Cross the line if you dare
This is one screwed up place here
A shattered part of living
You just can't . . . repair
Sunny day, on the way
Silly moon, clown wants to play
An unwanted shadow
Covers all of me
Keeps me from being
Who I want to be
The damned black
That's all I can see
The demon controls me

The Battle Cry

The Battle Cry
Fell a bit too shy
Of the force the king had hoped for

Still, sturdy in might
To take to the fight
The soldiers marched across the moor

The fog sat low
Something hiding below
The enemy, unseen laid in wait

The cries of Valhalla
Up high, flew the banner
As the king's men rushed to heaven's gate

At the crest of the hill
The blood started to spill
As the troops crashed into each other

All screams and cries
No one could recognize
Of their brethren who fell asunder

By axe or by sword
By cutting or being gored
Only bloody madmen left to pray

Like present, war is still used today
The battles of blood always stay
Just new updated methods to slay

We continue using war again
To kill children, women and men
Why don't we learn from the King's battle past?

There can be no thrills, just shrills
In finding new weapons that kill
Death agents when ordered, don't relent

One day we'll face our mistakes
As our sun rises and wakes
We will slay all ourselves and the moor will be silent

Dying Leaves

The passing season shall be set free
Like the falling leaves from the tree
Where do the leaves go?
Wherever the wind blows

Fall, the amazing color
Reflects a promise of light
Bless the magic light!
Images I'll carry tonight

Beauty, intoxicating shades
Cyclic whimsy in the fall
Resilient life as death fades
Like mighty trees standing tall

In the air, floats a majestic hymn
Soon, the moon begins to rise
Colored leaves nearby, I collect them
To wax, to remember and to prize

Perfect Match

Like our sunlit ocean that crashes on the beach
With its lofty fingers and outward reach
I call out to you to remember the time we first met
How our hearts pounded at our each and every breath

Oh, magical evenings, soon to follow
Private interludes by our secret tree hollow
All that life had to offer, the "us" could provide
We chose each other for we knew each other inside

Soul mates from the start, this was certainly clear
Our eyes connected and washed away any fear
Our matched lips molded so perfectly well
When we finally kissed and held each other in a spell

I captured your essence and lived in your heart
You captured my life force and we would never be apart

Bernkastel Kues!

There are no "Grapes of Wrath."
Just seedlings covering the hill
As the sun rises and reveals them
They are still
A sweet, yet sour smell wafts around
The smell of over-ripe cuts, on the ground
Cast along the Mosel river bend
A river seemingly with no end
Small villages line the shore
A mile or two in size, no more
Above, in the highs a castle
A castle of old and tales of lore
I can see an oversized oak door
The entrance, no doubt
Beyond the stronghold and lookout
Clear, clear blue skies
Tree-lined horizon adds to the view
This image forever emblazoned on my mind
One of countless places I've seen
A magic I could never forget . . . so serene
A treasure to hold and forever endear
No, no "Grapes of Wrath," here!

When Are We All Going To Care?

Eggs gone bad
Cow's gone mad!
Bio-genetics gone wrong
Simple virus comes along
World is growing
Census numbers showing
Too many to feed
Some won't eat till they need
So, what's the plan?
Continue to mettle
New ingredients in the kettle
But, what to do
To feed a simple few
Who wander by day?
Nightly, no place to stay
Others die from disease
Vaccines are scant for these
One dollar for a mosquito net
Many don't care, or just forget
Some say Americans first
Let the other countries thirst
Some who live well
Shall die in their made hell
Many will see the light
They care about the other's plight
Myself, I try to do what's right
"I" will sleep soundly tonight
DNA, crossbreeds and shots

Those that have and the have-nots
Creeping pollution we don't see
Kills us indiscriminately
If you read this, you want to live
Do what's right, love and give
Even a simple dime
Will grow larger in time
Or, you can volunteer
Give time, time you can spare
The joy you will feel
Will make your life ideal!

Son's Rite of Passage

There's a place in life where all sons go
There's a time they change, all the things they've ever known
At a moment when it all comes rushing in
In a time when they don't know, if they end or if they begin

When a son turns to his dad and watches as he dies away

Nothing from then on, can ever be the same
There's only moments locked inside, the minds confusing game
All the color change from bright to a faded hue
Walk on tall and proud young man with all he's given you
Let the questions turn to answers and the answers come your way

When the son turns into the dad, weeping as his dad slips away

One day all will come to pass, a seething wound gone at last
Your time will come to make a stand, remember now you're past
Stand ever strong and firm but true
Yet humble man that you've become, must remember too
One day there will be neither questions nor answers there for you

It's a standard rite of passage
In a time of deep despair
As the boatman rows to shore
To remind us he is there
The siren's song is singing
As the reaper hones his scythe
To alert us, one day we must commit

Till Then:

Let the sun shine in her glory
Let God's birds sing songs of praise
Free the ships from their moorings
Let them ride the crashing waves
On to yonder, let us push on
Bring us home, to safe and warm
Let a new day ring with passion
Give us peace and hope and calm

Leaving winter

The ice cracks under my feet
A time when winter will soon cease
A horrid time of year some say
I, I agree in a way, but
The sky is majesty
A church steeple rises high above me
In the distant forest I can hear silence
A curious silence, a wondrous zone
What a blessed man I am to own
This time alone with my trusty dog
A moment worthy of logging, so I pen
Never a similar moment shall happen again

Cold Justice

Taught, stiff, waiting
Hallway, marble, railing
Stairway to nowhere
Pillars rise high
Twenty eight glass windows
Leading to the outside
Towering building
Courtyard that shows
Brick laden walkway
Three stories below
Roped off sections
Like that of a theater
For this is a theater of fear
The justice, law presides here
People poised everywhere
Some just suddenly appear
They walk by you
Some report "how do you do"?
Knowing this is not a positive place
There is much bad energy here
If it weren't for my situation
I would choose to be elsewhere

My God's Comfort

A moment of scars
One lifetime apart
Passing on by the trees
Staring without their leaves
I'm falling to my knees

My God with comfort brings
Sometimes we lose our bearings
Powerless and fragile
Precious time, broken still
Whilst my God's blood spills

Conceded in struggle
Indifferent and little
All needless control
Just best not to know
My God seeds us to grow

Quiet is a friend
No one there to offend
Gives a means to an end
Striking a noiseless bargain
Falling to my knees again
From my God, I am

Nature Always Brings

Let the rain wash over us each
Wash away our troubles with our tears
Gentle cooling waters from the air
Soothing drops falling resound in my ears

Darkest days of November don't last
The sun will rise once again, light bright
To warm the earth covered in dreadful frostbite!
Sparkling moisture rising to star filled, clear nights

As we snuggle in blankets and pillows in bed
Dream sleeping babies of wonderful things
Like resonating crystals and golden rings
Round colorful rainbows and all that life brings

Multi-colored skies may your magic touch every soul
Wash away negatives and set us each free
Fill our dreams with your sweet liquid candy
Cover us in possibility of whatever can be

Fault Kills

It's the fault
That kills
One can't see
What's coming
Blind man walking
Someone is talking
Who broke the feeling?
Trust, once was healing
9.5, on the Richter scale
Dead on the streets
It goes away, each day
The feelings that keep
It's the fault
That disintegrates
Who made the promise?
A lie you can't hide
Blame denies ownership
Pointing a finger
Makes misery linger
Wasted time is rot
Could it be their fault?
It's not

Gyroscope

Perpetual motion
Of seeking dope
Of course, alcohol
Then, the fall
Hard to recall
Go with the spin
Reclusive sin
Have to take it in
Need to spit it out
Still going around
One foot on the ground
Can't find the other
So what, whatever
Takes you where it will
Refuses to spill
Always a thrill
Bump and then go
Your universe a flow
At the edge now
"Lookout below"

Hidden Emotions

She sits on her throne with a book
By a dimly lit lamp giving light
She gives a poor man a simple look
With a smile like the sun, so bright!

But, something behind her visible eyes
A glimpse of confusion and pain
Perhaps at night she reflects and cries
For a hurt she can no longer sustain

Comfortable in a chair with a pillow
Lost in a book of some fictional story
Perhaps she is dreaming of pussy-willows
And a place of butterflies and morning glory

One can see strength in her face
Brown hair soft and subtle lines
A confident purpose in place
What a man desires, she defines

A moment will pass and change will take place
The poor man she eyes now is leaving
She puts down the fiction and covers her face
For in real life, she is grieving

www.ingramcontent.com/pod-product-compliance
Ingram Content Group UK Ltd.
Pitfield, Milton Keynes, MK11 3LW, UK
UKHW040601210726
13854UKWH00008B/1706

9 781463 413811